Deliver

*How to Perform Your Best
When it Counts the Most*

By Josh Matthews-Morgan
and
Dr. Nita Matthews-Morgan

Mind Matters International

Table of Contents

Why Hermes?

We wrote this book to describe the universal principles that guide successful performers. We wanted a powerful image for our cover that would symbolize performance of all types. And who better to embody the message of our book than the Greek god, Hermes? In Greek mythology, Hermes was the god of speech, sports and commerce. He was the protector and guide of performers in many fields, including athletes, actors, speakers, and businesspeople.

This book is a modern-day guide for all performers seeking to master the inner game of their craft.

"There is a vitality, a life force, a quickening that is translated through you into action, and because there is only one of you in all time, this expression is unique. And if you block it, it will never exist through any other medium, and it will be lost. The world will not have it. It is not your business to determine how good it is, nor how valuable, nor how it compares with other expressions. It is your business to keep it yours clearly and directly, to keep the channel open."

Martha Graham, legendary choreographer and dancer

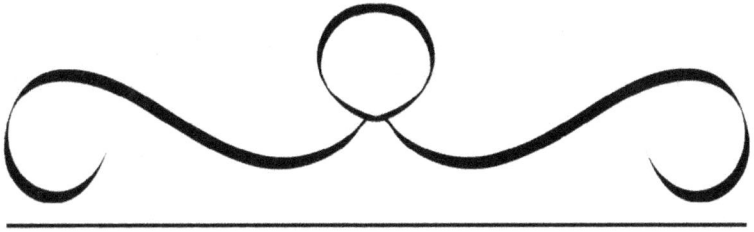

Prologue:
David's Story

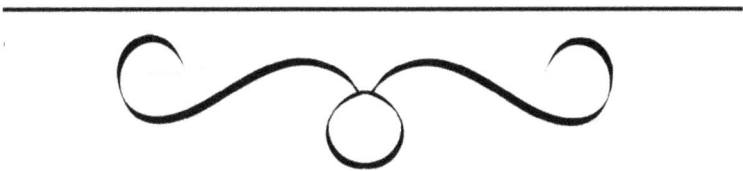

D avid shifted nervously in his seat. He wiped his palms on his pants, first looking to see if anyone was watching him. The truth was that he was more nervous than he had ever been in his life, and it felt like the wait was taking forever.

He silently rehearsed the opening words of the speech he was about to give: *We knew when we started this project that we were onto something great...* In his head, the words flowed naturally. Still, he felt the sinking sensation in his stomach deepen the closer it got to his time to present.

He couldn't help but replay in his mind the strange turn of events that had led him to be sitting there, sharing the stage with all the bigwigs of his firm. As sales manager for one of the largest pharmaceutical companies in the world, he had been asked six months ago to lead a special project with his team. Sales had been down for months, and the whole sales force had slipped into a negative funk. Fingers were pointed in blame. People questioned the direction of the company, the way they went about selling their products to hospitals and doctors' offices across the country.

He was given a special assignment to turn his team around, which people in the know jokingly referred to as "Project Hope." He was supposed to lead the charge back, to show everybody that business would rebound if they followed a certain protocol and executed it successfully, as he knew they could.

After five months, it was obvious that he was onto something, because sales were up dramatically within his team, far surpassing anything the other sales teams had achieved. But he didn't know how ecstatic his superiors were about his work until he was called into the CEO's office, a man he had spoken to only in passing in the ten years he had been working there. "David, you did a hell of a job with Project Hope," the famously hardnosed CEO told him. "We're really proud of you."

David stammered something about how it was a team effort, that he didn't deserve all the credit, but he was immediately cut off. "David, we're so happy with the results of this little project that I want you to tell the whole company about it. Next week, as you know, we're having our conference in Minneapolis. I'm going to make you the featured speaker. Y'know, fire up the troops. Give them something to..." he paused to emphasize the next word, "*hope* for." Laughing at his own cleverness, he continued. "After that, I'm going to send you to all the divisions and you're going to show them what you've done. You're going to help get this company back on track."

In his shock, David remembered only a few words here and there from his boss's monologue—words like "promotion," "star," and "exactly what we needed."

So here he was, about to give the biggest speech of his life. But he had never felt comfortable speaking to big audiences. Sure, he was funny and personable when he was with his friends, always quick to crack a joke and lighten the mood. But he wasn't the same person when he was speaking in front of an audience. It was as if the connections from his brain to his mouth were shut down. He silently hoped that this time would be different, that he would nail the speech. Too much was riding on it for him to fail. In his mind, his career depended on him being successful in these next few moments.

The sound of his name derailed his train of thought: The emcee was introducing him. In a moment, he would be in the spotlight. Hundreds of people from his company, hundreds of his coworkers, friends and people he barely knew, would sit there before him, judging the content of his performance for the next fifteen minutes. He silently prayed that he would deliver, just as he did on Project Hope.

As he walked up to the podium, he felt his throat tighten and go dry. He paused for a moment to try to pull himself together, and when he began to speak, his voice sounded foreign, like it was coming out of some other person's mouth. "When we started this project, we knew it was going to be a lot of fun…" Damn, he was already off track. His mind frantically tried to find the words he had carefully rehearsed, but they were gone. He laughed nervously, hoping the crowd would join him, but an army of impassive faces stared back at him.

The next fifteen minutes were the longest of his life. David managed to get through his speech, but only after rambling and getting off track several times. He felt off balance up there, like a fish out of water. All the jokes he had carefully inserted into his speech seemed to backfire. Even after hours of preparation, he couldn't get comfortable on the stage, couldn't get into the flow.

The audience applauded politely when his speech mercifully came to an end. David felt dejected and tried to hide his disappointment when he shook the emcee's hand and turned the mike back over to him. But the damage had already been done. *The entire company just watched me make a fool of myself,* he thought. He couldn't escape the irony: The man who had so confidently led his team to great success in sales had been reduced to a blathering idiot, just when he needed to nail his speech.

That night, as he replayed those agonizing 15 minutes on stage, David wondered what he could have done differently. It wasn't that he hadn't prepared for it: he'd memorized his notes and practiced in front of the mirror dozens of times. He just couldn't get into his groove when he faced all those people. But he'd seen others shine, right in the moment when it counted the most. What was their secret sauce?

With a lump in his throat, he realized that he would be speaking over and over again to the different divisions about the project. *If I don't get better at speaking,* he thought, *it's going to be a long year.* In that moment, David promised himself that he would find a way to become a speaker who could really deliver.

How to Use This Book

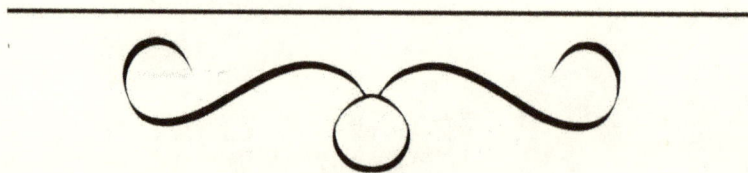

You have picked up this book because, like David, you are a performer of some kind. You might be uncomfortable calling yourself a "performer," thinking that word should be reserved for only professional artists and musicians—people who make a living standing on the stage. But the truth is that we have all been performers at some point; we've all had times when we had to put our best foot forward while being evaluated by others.

And as a performer, you are probably aware of the critical role your mental state plays in your performance. You've experienced times when nothing went right no matter how hard you tried and times when everything seemed to flow.

Every word in this book has been carefully crafted to put you into a peak state of performance, where you access a version of yourself that is truly awe-inspiring, insightful, and incredibly capable and talented. No doubt, you have discovered this version of yourself from time to time in your daily life. You might have even experienced it during those times when you performed, when you felt as if, for a brief period of time, your words and actions would take on an elevated importance.

This book is based on a simple premise: that whether your performance is in the arts or in athletics, in sales or on the stage, the mental process that will put you in the space where truly awe-inspiring deeds can take place is one and the same.

When you get down to the essence of what separates peak performers in any field from those who don't live up to their potential, you begin to see that these peak performers are able to access a very similar mindset. The doubts that keep the salesperson from really stepping into her power are the same worries and doubts that keep the musician and the athlete from being the awe-inspiring performers that they are capable of being. The negative mental chatter that blocks the public speaker's words from flowing with ease is the same noise that actually downshifts the body and dulls the athlete's mind on the field.

To be certain, your performance will look different if you are about to perform in your first concert than if you are about to have the biggest sales meeting of your life. We are not suggesting that your best performance will look anything like someone else's from the outside, nor do we want it to. What we are suggesting is that your best performance comes when you connect with the purest and most powerful essence of who you are and what you have to give.

When you're at your best, you have access to all of your best resources: honed mind and body, creative ideas, accumulated knowledge. There is an easy connection between your thoughts and actions as they coordinate to bring your best self forward. Your thoughts align and your body functions at its best. You are not distracted by the chatter in your mind—you perform in a bubble of time so contained that you concentrate all your power and potential in the present. You feel calm as you experience yourself performing beyond your expectations. In short, you are at your best.

The ideas in this book are only half the equation for getting you to your best performance, however; practice and preparation are the other half. We cannot overstate the importance of these two ingredients for your successful performance.

You may think of practicing as the bitter pill you have to swallow to get the applause and the accolades, but we want you to learn to enjoy your practice. Enjoy the feeling of getting better, of constantly improving and reaching toward the best version of you. The fun of the entire process is in your personal evolution, in surpassing your previous best.

Practice brings with it a major benefit: If you practice anything long enough, it becomes automatic. Your mental energy reserve is freed up to help you think on your feet so that you can creatively deal with any new challenge.

As for the second ingredient, there is, unfortunately, no magic potion that can help you perform at your best without thoroughly preparing for that performance. You would be foolish to show up for a sales meeting without getting your ducks in a row. Preparing for it will give you the advantage of knowing what you need to know so that you can relax when it's time for you to deliver.

We suggest that you read this book as part of your preparation, but know that it was not written to be read one time through and put back on the shelf. Performance is a process that you will be continuously refining, and with that in mind, we intentionally made each section short and easily accessible so you can find the ideas that will best serve you in any particular situation.

Our suggestion for you: Read this book from front to back the first time, as you would any other book. Relax as you read; absorb the words, and let them sink into your mind. Then, after you are familiar with the basic flow, be selective about which sections you read.

If you have time before your performance, take a few minutes to browse through the chapters. Some sections of this book will call to you more than others at any given time. For instance, sometimes your greatest challenge will be detaching yourself from the outcome of your performance, while at other times you may want to let go of what others think so you can be at your best. With time and continued exposure to the ideas contained in this book, you will find yourself internalizing these ideas and living by them, easily reaching your personal state of peak performance.

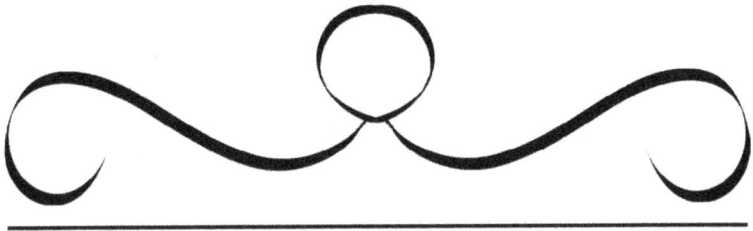

Let Go of the Outcome

"Success means doing the best we can with what we have. Success is the doing, not the getting; in the trying, not the triumph. Success is a personal standard, reaching for the highest that is in us, becoming all that we can be."

Zig Ziglar, author, salesman, and motivational speaker

Detaching yourself from the outcome will lead you to great performances. When you most need to win or succeed, you're sunk. There's something about psychologically freeing yourself up to be okay no matter how it turns out that gives you the greatest strength when you need it most.

There's a big difference between wanting to perform well and needing to perform well. You can't access the resources of your pure desire if you *need* something to happen. Needing a particular outcome puts you in a "one-down" position that doesn't give you access to the best version of you. You might believe that you need something to happen, that something huge is riding on your performance, that this moment is the defining moment of your life or career. But you certainly can't think like that if you want to perform at your best.

This might sound like sacrilege to you, but forget about how it turns out. Forget everything you know about succeeding or failing, winning and losing, and just do, just express. Doing badly or well has nothing to do with your personal worth, only with the mental state you are in. Take the pressure off yourself that you have to be perfect, and then the perfection can shine through.

Sometimes, when you are thinking "positively" about the result that you want, you're really adding extra pressure. Thinking "I have to hit a home run," or even "I have to get this deal," is putting the cart before the horse. Let the results take care of themselves.

Performance is a process. Burn this into your mind: Consistently getting the results you want is about consistently mastering the steps, not trying to force every outcome. See yourself mastering the process and giving your undivided attention to being so good at this particular moment that the results take care of themselves. Don't worry about getting there. You'll get to amazing places if you follow this rule: Let go of the destination and enjoy the journey.

When you let go of the outcome, then it will turn out the way you want it. You aren't there for the accolades, or to impress anybody; you are there to be the perfect expression of your best and highest performance, to allow it to happen for your benefit and for the benefit of others.

The outcome you want is within your reach, but in order to reach it, you have to let it go. It's the paradox of performance: The less you care about the outcome and the need to perform well, the better you do perform.

Detach from your need to be really good. Just be you. And attach yourself to this moment.

Of course, really getting into this moment is a lot easier when you...

Ignore the Peanut Gallery

"I'm not in this world to live up to your expectations, and you're not in this world to live up to mine."

Bruce Lee, actor, martial artist, film director

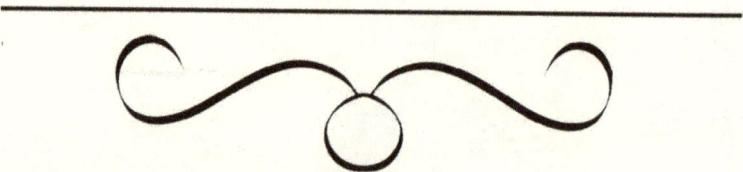

Win or lose, succeed or fail, what other people think of you and your performance is completely irrelevant. It's none of your business. You are not there to impress them. In fact, the more impressive you try to be, the less impressive you end up being. Let go of the peanut gallery, which is any opinion that isn't your own, and discover the inner strength that resides within you at all times.

If someone finds you lacking in some way, know that it is their own lack of perspective on your value that is causing their discomfort. Even with the most spectacular, seemingly flawless performance, there are those people who will look for the faults, who will find phantom mistakes to complain about. Know that the real flaw is in their thinking, not in anything that you have done. The harshest critic is constantly fighting against his own internal critic.

You can't allow the expectations of others to tarnish your true brilliance. Their expectations stem from what is going on inside their own head, and those expectations are usually pretty unrealistic. Get out of their head and get firmly into your own.

Our tendency is to want everybody to agree about our own brilliance. But you cannot make someone else happy with anything you do. The way they feel about you is their choice; their happiness is their choice. Some people are impossible to please, and the best thing you can do for yourself, and for your performance, is to stop trying to please them. You don't need the approval of your mother, your father, or any judge, fan, or committee evaluating you from a distance. You don't need the world to think that you are the best at what you do, because the world cannot agree on anything. You don't need them to sign off on who you are to be validated. Validate yourself. If they don't like it, it's their problem and not yours. You have absolutely nothing to prove to anybody, so stop trying.

Let go of the impossible task of winning the vote of everybody around you and you'll discover a much grander truth: When you don't care about impressing anyone, you allow the truly impressive qualities you possess to emerge. Someone may notice them, in time. But it doesn't matter that a single person cannot see them. Your performance isn't about impressing other people—the "peanut gallery." That's just a natural consequence of you being at your best. Your performance is about yourself, not about them.

When you truly don't care about other peoples' opinions, it frees you to...

Be Authentically You

"Always be a first-rate version of yourself instead of a second-rate version of someone else."

Judy Garland, actress and singer

You don't need to perform like anybody else. In fact, you can't perform like anybody else. You don't benefit anyone by regurgitating what has worked for someone else. There are a million different paths to a successful outcome, and you can easily get lost following other people's road maps.

Know this: What has worked for someone else is not necessarily what will work for you. Their path to a successful performance was a result of their own unique combination of desire, talent, and personality. Like it or not, you must blaze your own trail.

The quickest way to shoot yourself in the foot is to compare yourself to others. It's easy to look at the greats in your field and to hero-worship, to think, "I could never do that." And you're right—you could never repeat what they've done. But you aren't here to repeat anything. Their performance, their greatness, was an expression of their inner potential. Your greatness, the expression of your own inner potential, will be crafted on completely different terms.

Compare yourself to others only when looking for inspiration. The performance of the greats can serve to inspire you; it can plant a seed in your mind of how great you can be, what you are capable of achieving. It's your job to nurture that seed so that your own image of your success grows. Become that image, letting it come forth in your own unique, authentic way.

When things are going badly, you'll want to hear other people's opinions about what to fix, and most people will be happy to tell you what they think you should do differently. Absorb only the advice that resonates with you, the advice that feels right to you. If it takes you off your center, if it feels like someone else's path, let it go. Don't evaluate what other people suggest using your head and your logic, because they can mislead you. An idea can make a lot of sense to you intellectually and sound great in your head, but still not be right for you.

Instead, evaluate every suggestion against your inner knowing, at your heart level. A suggestion is only helpful when it clicks in that place inside of you that knows the truth of what you are considering. Only you can truly know what you need to find your balance.

You must learn to stay within yourself if you want to create a truly great performance. You must learn to be authentically and decisively you.

And expressing your authentic performance happens when you...

Set a Strong Intention

"If fame is your primary goal, you undermine the motivation required to become truly great... Greatness takes unbridled passion for the task at hand, which means pure motivation. If you play for passion, you play for fun. You don't care what others think, you play because you want to, like kids playing baseball in the backyard. That is the essence of pure motivation."

Dr. Michael Lardon, sports psychiatrist and author of Finding Your Zone: 10 Core Lessons for Peak Performance in Sports and Life

Your intention sets the boundaries for your individual achievement. Make it strong, and amaze yourself with what you can do. Weaken it, dilute it with thoughts of need and lack, and watch as you lose your luster when the lights are brightest.

Be aware of why you want what you want. Intention is the ending to the statement: "I want to do this thing because..." Or "I want to be the best because..."

Weak intention is what you get when you perform for others, when you do it to impress people or for the acclaim. It's the voice within that says you have to prove something to someone. It gets you thinking ahead; it's what happens when you get caught up in the rat race of trying to figure out what your performance will *mean* in the eyes of others. It's getting excited about seeing that plaque on the wall while dreading what it will take to get there.

Strong intention is what you get when you perform for yourself, for the thrill of performance. It calls forth the best in you and gets you excited about a higher purpose. It energizes your mind and propels you into action. It excites you with the knowledge of what you're capable of, the knowledge that you can do something you have never before achieved. Strong intention can be felt by others at a deep, emotional level, and it allows them to feel the power of your being expressing itself. A strong intention allows you to enjoy the journey of performance as a discovery of the hidden treasure within.

When you were a kid playing in the sandbox, you built castles not to prove that you could make the biggest and baddest castle around. You didn't do it to be known as the best castle maker. You jumped in headfirst because you loved the process of creation, because it was fun to build something from the ground up and to see it take place before your very eyes. Get back to the fun. Find the thrill of performance again and that feeling will carry you farther than you could ever expect.

The strongest intention you can hold is to be the fullest expression of you in this moment. You have to fall in love with the idea of performing at your best for the selfish reason of loving the journey. That kind of intention spurs you on to greatness because it summons inner resources that you didn't even know you had to help you.

When that is your intention, magic happens. Your mind, body and actions align to create a truly sublime experience. And then the funniest thing happens: People start to take notice. You are at your best and it becomes undeniable to those watching you. They'll ask you what your magic is, what secret sauce you take. And if you keep your intention pure, you'll smile and appreciate their appreciation, but it won't be something you need.

Your performance is about getting to your highest and best form of expression in this moment.

Setting this pure intention will drive you to your best performance and allow you to...

Find Your Confidence

"What lies behind us and what lies before us are tiny matters compared to what lies within us."

Ralph Waldo Emerson, essayist, lecturer and poet

Confidence is the reflection of an inner awareness of your value. It's not something you have after you psych yourself up in the mirror. It's not the words that you speak to yourself out loud. Confidence comes from within. It's there all the time, even if you're not aware of it.

You don't need to have confidence in a particular skill to have confidence in yourself as a person. Consider this: You are already naturally confident. The only reason you might not have access to your full confidence, even after you've prepared, is because you are blocking it. The good news is that you don't have to do anything to be more confident. Confidence is what happens when you let go of the thoughts that are keeping you from being confident.

The thought that you have to be perfect will keep you from feeling confident. If you have to be perfect before you perform, you will never get on the stage or in the boardroom. Use your perfect attention to details when you're getting ready for your performance, but when it's your turn at bat, allow yourself to give your best, even if you think it's not perfect. You will surprise yourself when you relax even if you don't feel entirely confident.

When you are anxious or worried about your performance, it means that you are thinking about the future, or thinking about how other people will judge your performance. All of that is wasted mental energy. Focus on what you are here to do now. Center yourself in the value you have to offer and your worry will melt away. Trust that you are prepared for any obstacle that might present itself, that you can handle it with the same ease with which you walk and talk.

If this is your first rodeo, you're probably not going to have as much confidence in the task at hand as the seasoned professional. Don't worry if you can't find the feeling of confidence; you've succeeded in the past, so be grounded in that confidence and borrow it for this new event.

If it's your first time on the horse, don't wait for confidence to show up. That comes from doing it. It's a lie that you have to feel confidence before you reach your goals or reach peak performance. Your body and words can project confidence even if your mind isn't there yet. Just show up and eventually your mind will catch up.

All your preparation serves for one thing: so that you will confidently knock it out of the ballpark. Even if you didn't prepare up to your own standards for whatever reason, you can still find the feeling of confidence.

Some people prepare relentlessly for their performance, yet they shake when the time comes to deliver. Others put much less effort in and somehow manage to excel. The difference between the two? The second person found the feeling of confidence more quickly—and it's ultimately the *feeling* of confidence that translates into an outstanding performance.

Your feeling of confidence can become second nature when you learn to consistently...

Center Yourself in Your Value

"Your playing small does not serve the world. There is nothing enlightened about shrinking so that other people won't feel insecure around you. We are all meant to shine, as children do. We were born to make manifest the glory of God that is within us. It's not just in some of us; it's in everyone. And as we let our own light shine, we unconsciously give other people permission to do the same. As we are liberated from our own fear, our presence automatically liberates others."

Marianne Williamson, lecturer, best-selling author and spiritual activist

There are always people who can benefit from your performance, but don't feel that you are responsible at all for the course of their lives. Still, be aware that your performance can have a life-changing impact on others as they experience you at your best.

Think back to a time when you felt deeply touched by the presence and power of another person. Remember when your mouth dropped in awe at what you saw someone else do, when you felt the ripple of excitement coursing through your body and you knew that you had just witnessed a special moment. What you felt was the outer expression of inner value. It was the authentic performance of someone who was at the top of their game, someone who knew that her performance was a gift to everyone close by.

Truly awe-inspiring performances happen when you connect to that deep core of value that you possess. Like an explosion, the shock waves of your presence and power reverberate inside everyone around you. When you reach for that deep core of value, you have enormous power to influence events and circumstances. You become the center of attention. It's as if everything else is flowing around you. Your presence is commanding and undeniable. People naturally defer to you. It's like you have summoned a tidal wave of energy that carries everybody and everything in its path toward their greatest good.

Notice what you do well and the strengths you bring to the table. Focus on them and watch as they grow right before your eyes. Your weaknesses are not weaknesses unless you think of them as such. Right before you perform is not the time to browse through your failures, those times when you fell short of what you intended. Instead, it is the

33

time to center yourself on the value that you bring. Learn from those mistakes what you must, and then focus only on your success.

At your core, you bring enormous value to this interaction and to this experience. After all, you are unrepeatable. No one else on this Earth has the unique collection of genes, experiences and skills that you bring to this present moment and circumstance. Apply that uniqueness to this moment.

When you connect to your core of value, you have more to give others. You can influence others to shine in that same way, so that you all uplift each other. A tiny pebble dropped in the pond can set off ripples that travel across the entire lake. Be the pebble.

This feeling of value will lead you to....

Expect Success

"If you believe you can, you probably can. If you believe you won't, you most assuredly won't. Belief is the ignition switch that gets you off the launching pad."

Denis Waitley, best-selling author, motivational speaker and expert on peak performance

Your performance always matches what you expect at your deepest level—not the fleeting thoughts about what would be nice to do, but what you *believe* you can do. Clear belief sharpens the mind, drives you into action, and ultimately creates your performance.

What you think about, talk about, and imagine are powerful predictors of your performance. The stories you tell yourself and others actually shape what you expect for the future. If you insist on talking about your past in realistic terms, describing how you fell short of your best, you can assure yourself of more of the same. You might think that repeatedly talking about your performance in an honest way helps you, but don't kid yourself. All of your "now" stories feed into one another to literally create your future performances.

Your expectation drives your body and mind into action. Expectation has a way of acting through you and others to create what you believe deep down. If you don't have the belief that everything is always working out for you, then you have to overcompensate with your actions and force things to happen. If you don't expect things to turn out for the best, you easily slip into the "try hard" mode, which takes you out of the flow. But no matter how hard you try, your outcomes will usually fall into the realm of what you believe you're capable of, how you "know" things will turn out at the deepest level.

If you feel that your thoughts are out of whack, that you're expecting the worst or something less than the best, know that you can change it. Your expectation is the thought that you hold all the time about your performance. Practice holding another thought, and watch as things change before your eyes.

Give absolutely no mental energy to what could go wrong, or to how you might not be in the right place at the right time, or to any reason why you might not be successful, yadda yadda. That's what we call "arguing for your limitations," coming up with all the reasons something might not work out. That kind of mind game will keep you stuck performing at a level that doesn't satisfy you.

Instead, argue for your success. Argue for how you always excel at what you do, regardless of your history. When you get to the place of thinking only about performing at your best, then your success will be undeniable. Mohammed Ali's trainer, Angelo Dundee, wrote a book with one of the most brilliant titles ever: *I Only Talk Winning*. Take a page from his book and talk and think only about your successful performance. Why expect anything less?

Believe that you are good, that you deserve the best, and that things are always turning out well for you, and they will. If you don't expect the best, you're not giving the best version of yourself a chance to show up and assist you.

But even when you are expecting success, you can get yourself in trouble. When in doubt, it's always best to...

Keep it Simple

"Simplicity is the final achievement. After one has played a vast quantity of notes and more notes, it is simplicity that emerges as the crowning reward of art."

Frederic Chopin, composer and virtuoso pianist

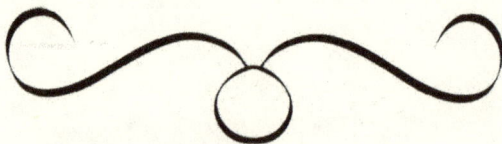

Usually, the most brilliant performances feature the most simplified approaches. The idea that more is better is not always true, especially in performance. It's not that you are dumbing it down, or making it less powerful; on the contrary, there's an elegance and beauty to something that's simple.

Your tendency will likely be to want to clutter things up with more stuff. Don't do that. Don't try to do something outside of your realm of comfort. The time to experiment and expand your horizons happens during your preparation. Your performance should come as simply and as naturally as tying your shoes.

When you keep it simple, you can focus more. You don't try to juggle too many things at once or cloud the issue with unnecessary stuff. Take away all of those moving parts and strip it down to the basics, to the most essential steps for your success, to the things that you are already doing with ease. You don't need to get too fancy to impress anybody when you perform.

Underlying the feeling of making things too complicated is the feeling that you're not enough, or that you aren't ready enough. Know that you are prepared, you are ready. Trust in your preparation, in the fact that you are at this stage for a reason. You already excel at what you do. Own it, and know that it's all happening in perfect timing.

You get in trouble when you start second-guessing your approach at the last minute. In fact, the biggest danger is not that you have chosen the wrong approach. The biggest danger is in waffling, in doubting what you have already carved out, in wondering if there might be a better way, in

Keep it Simple

splitting your energy with self-doubt.

Make the decision that you're going to go for it with what
you've got, and that it's enough. You don't need to throw
out your approach at the last minute. You don't need to
add extra layers of complication to what you have already
achieved. The last minute is not the time to be perfecting
what you do, it's the time to relax and let it unfold. Your
hard work is behind you; now it's time to enjoy the fruits of
your labor by simply being at your best.

Keeping it simple has another great side effect—it makes
it easier to...

Control What You Can Control

"Nothing splendid has ever been achieved except by those who dared believe that something inside of them was superior to circumstances."

Bruce Barton, author and U.S. Congressman

The simple reality is that the people who consistently perform at their highest levels have the most consistent mental control over themselves. Count yourself among the best by taking back your personal power and trying to control only the things you *can* control.

Most of us spend so much mental energy trying to control the things we can't control. Don't attempt the impossible—to force circumstances and people to bend to your wishes. Instead, embrace the idea of what you yourself are all about. Things don't have to line up perfectly for you to be at your best; your best is a moment-by-moment state that you can achieve under any conditions. Learn to thrive in any situation by controlling what you can control: your thoughts, feelings and actions.

When you worry about those dreaded circumstances that you can't control, you split your energy in different directions. Your energy is a precious resource for your peak performance, but only if it is strong and focused. Splitting your energy is like trying to drive with the emergency brake on: all that power under the hood is held back, unable to work for you. You can step on the gas all you want, but you won't get up to your top speed. Feel the true freedom of letting go of what you can't control and giving everything you've got to what you can control.

Just as blaming your circumstances won't allow you to shine, giving others either the credit or the blame for your performance is a form of personal bondage. Some people spend a lifetime in the mental prison of allowing others to have power over their performance. The plain and simple fact is this: it is always you doing the performance. Others can influence you into a different space of performance, for better or for worse, but you are the one allowing them to influence you. As Zig Ziglar says, "You are the only person on Earth who can use your ability."

What are the things you can't control? What other people think and feel, whether they like you and approve of you, how they react to you, and how they act. You can't control the conditions in which you perform, including the weather, having your equipment break down when you most need it, or how your competition shows up.

What you can control: your thoughts, feelings and actions—how you respond to any conditions or circumstances.

See yourself in such complete control over what you can control—yourself—that your performance unfolds in exactly the way you want it to.

Gain control of yourself and you will find that the power of your influence is enormous. You will find that while you can't change conditions, you can make them nearly irrelevant to your success. Get to the place of *knowing* that you can thrive regardless of what's going around you, and you will arrive at the true pinnacle of performance.

Control what you can control and it will turn out the way you want more often than not. If it doesn't go your way, though, the best thing you can do is...

Make Peace with Failure

"I've missed more than 9,000 shots in my career. I've lost almost 300 games. Twenty-six times I've been trusted to take the game-winning shot and missed. I've failed over and over and over again in my life. And that is why I succeed."

Michael Jordan, NBA Hall of Fame basketball player

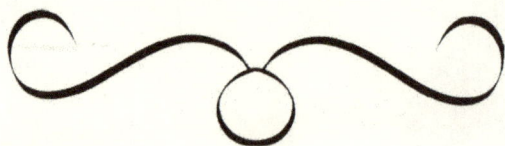

Learn to start making peace with what you consider "failure," and you'll free yourself up to be at your best. When you see failure for what it really is—the first step on your way to success—then you'll gain faster access to your best performance.

Most performers focus their mental energy more on the fear of failing than on the pleasure of excelling. Intense fear of failure is a ball and chain that keeps you from your best performance. That's because you can't have the fear of failure and the love of doing your best within you at the same time; that would be like feeling both depressed and happy at once.

It might help you to realize that some of the people who succeed the most have also failed the most in their lives. When you see the greats performing with incredible ease, you might feel there is no way you could ever get there. But the version you are seeing of them now is not how they always were. What you're seeing now is the result of persistent practice and a strong vision of their success.

Know that they probably started out struggling mightily. In most cases, the people who struggle the most and the hardest at the beginning are the same people who later learn to master their art. The difference between them and those who fall short of their potential? Even at the height of their struggle, when things were going worse than they could imagine, they never lost sight of the vision of their supreme success. They *knew* on some deep heart level that their failures would sharpen them in the future, would make them wiser and smarter. They knew that it was only a matter of time before they put it all together. You can reach that same level of inner knowing by treating "failure" in the way it deserves.

The way you performed in the past has nothing to do with your performance now. The past will only affect your current performance if you let it. All of your past failures and successes have helped you build an image of the kind of performer you'd like to become. When you stumbled or "failed" in the past, it was really just you collecting data about how you want to perform in the future. All of that experience, good and bad, helped you create a version of yourself as a performer that is truly sublime. This version of you at the absolute top of your game can become a reality if you will step into it and let it happen.

Recognize that succeeding and failing are two sides of the same coin. Nobody has reached their peak performance in every single moment of their lives; every successful person has experienced the frustration of not performing at their best. In fact, part of performing is learning to stretch ourselves to greater levels of performance. It's the thrill of becoming more than we have been in the past, and we only become more after we fall down and scrape our knees.

Your best performance emerges when the fear of failure diminishes inside of you, when the idea of excelling thrills you more than falling short. Learn to make peace with "failing," and you will start really allowing your highest performances to shine through.

And if you still fear failure while you perform, mental peace can come when you successfully...

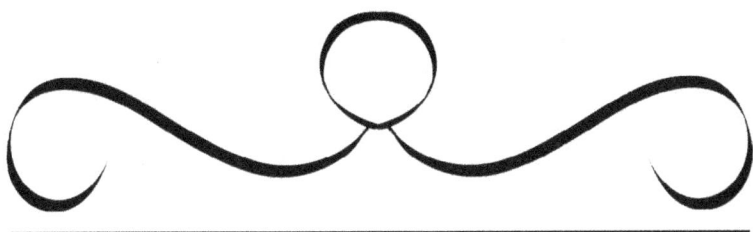

Detach From the Voice in Your Head

"Great works are done when one is not calculating and thinking."

Daisetz T. Suzuki, Buddhist and Zen philosopher and author

You need to have a quiet mind to access your best performance. Real freedom, flow and peak performance come when you can just observe yourself having a thought or feeling without getting caught up in it.

You have a voice in your head that's always talking to you. If you don't believe me, just listen to what it's saying right now as you're reading this. It's probably saying, "I'm not some crazy person who hears voices in my head!" That's your voice in your head.

This voice in your head never shuts up and it usually focuses on your mistakes. This voice will keep you out of flow and keep you from enjoying your performance. Most of the time, your inner voice is a mean bully that tries to whip you into shape by focusing on your faults and mistakes. These negative thoughts are your "head trash," your evaluations of yourself and others. Imagine if you talked to a beloved child the way you talk to yourself—can you see them being at their best hearing those words?

When you listen to your voice, you leave the present moment and travel down the rabbit hole of your mind. Think about when someone is talking to you and says something that strikes a nerve or reminds you of something you forgot to do: Off you go in your head, thinking about that tangent. You may be gone a second, a minute or even longer, but when you come back to the conversation, they're still talking and you don't know what the heck they said.

The same thing happens during your performance when you let your voice chatter on and on. You leave the present moment when you need to focus the most. What's happening to your performance while you're gone?

Your thoughts are like leaves flowing down a stream: When they get caught on branches, they pile up and slow the stream. With no obstructions in the way, they flow easily with the current. Just let your thoughts flow through you like leaves floating downstream; when thoughts come up during your performance, let them go.

You *can* get to the place where you simply observe your thoughts. You can critique and analyze your performance later, but now is not the time. Just detach from your thoughts; you will feel an instant relief and a connection to the moment. When you're connected to the moment, then you'll find flow.

Realize that your thoughts are not you; you are just having those thoughts. The real you is separate from the chatter in your brain. You are much grander than the fleeting thoughts zipping through your head, and that grander you emerges to help you when your mind is quiet, when you allow it to come forward. It's the shy face of your true nature, patiently waiting for your mind to be still so that it can awe you with its power.

Thoughts of worry about the outcome, or a need for perfection, make the real you vanish into thin air; they make you revert to the smaller, less connected, and less powerful version of you that stumbles.

Let go of those thoughts. When you get to that space of quiet, you have more power to perform at your best.

Detaching from your inner voice frees you to...

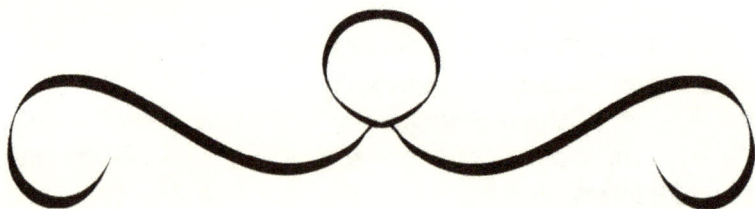

Give up Perfection

"I think perfectionism is based on the obsessive belief that if you run carefully enough, hitting each stepping-stone just right, you won't have to die. The truth is that you will die anyway and that a lot of people who aren't even looking at their feet are going to do a whole lot better than you, and have a lot more fun while they're doing it."

Anne Lamott, author and speaker

Perfection is doing your best in each moment. Your need for excellence drove you during your practice time to give your best and do your best. What you're looking for now is not a perfect performance: You're looking to relax and flow so you can perform at your best.

If you believe you have to be perfect, you're judging yourself by some screwy outward standard. There is no chart in the sky keeping track of your every step and judging you against some ideal of perfection. The reality is that no one has achieved perfection in everything. You can find a flaw in any performance.

The real problem is that you have a distorted view of yourself. We are all our own harshest critics, and that critical voice adds little to your performance. Other people aren't as demanding of you as your own internal voice is. The world is actually more accommodating than you think.

You might think that obsessing over a perfect outcome will help you get there. When you say to yourself, "I've got to be really great right now," it keeps you from being *here* right now, which keeps you from being great right now.

You might think that giving yourself commands that start with "I have to" and "I must" is a way to will yourself into a better performance. But it always backfires. The more you worry about the outcome and being "perfect," the less you focus on the process and the worse the outcome gets. Letting go of the outcome allows the process to carry you through.

Relax your own internal standards of perfection so you can get to your best at this moment. You've done your work, so allow yourself to be the fullest and best expression of who you are.

Connect with the perfection of each moment. Trust that all your previous work will show up at its best when you allow it to. Give up your need for perfection so you can be in flow.

Of course, this all happens naturally when you...

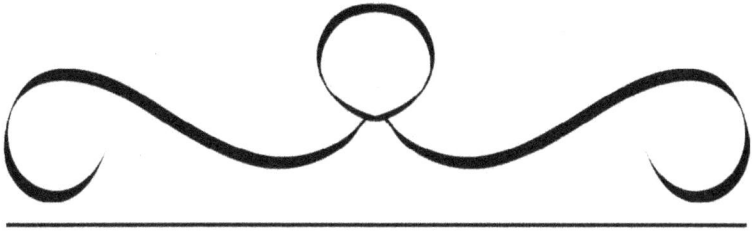

Embrace Anxiety

"Anxiety is the hand maiden of creativity."

T.S. Eliot, poet and playwright

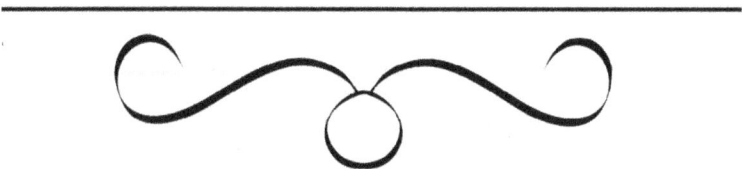

The more you fight your anxiety, the bigger it gets. You don't have to fear being anxious. After all, you need some anxiety for peak performance. Anxiety sharpens you, heightens your awareness, focuses your attention. Rest easy in it. That probably seems like a contradiction to you, but know this: When you worry about being anxious, you become more anxious.

You worry and fret because your amazing brain has been conditioned from the time of saber-toothed tigers to scan for danger and protect you. It's doing its job right now, only you don't have to let your anxiety control you.

Overwhelming anxiety zaps the precious mental energy that you need to stay focused. You only have so much energy for any situation, and negative feelings like worry, anger and frustration just deplete your energy stores. After all, you feel anxious because you are either jumping ahead to the future or you are wallowing in the past. You already know that worrying about the past or future doesn't help the present moment. All you have is this moment in time. Stay engaged in it. Stay engaged in the process. Stay in your awareness of each moment going into the next moment.

When you feel your anxiety rising, detach from it by separating yourself from your head chatter. Notice yourself feeling more anxious, and say, "I'm having the thought that I'm not good enough." Say, "Thank you, mind." Give your anxious voice a name: "There is Uncle Fred, telling me again that I won't be good enough for this task."

As soon as you name your feeling, you can distance yourself from it. You can remember that this voice is really not you, just some of your old head trash coming up. The real you is bigger than this voice, and this bigger you can recognize anxiety as the excitement that comes from stretching farther into your limitless self.

The real you wants this moment of performance so that you can show up in a grander way than ever before. Embrace anxiety and you'll get there.

Embracing anxiety gets you ready to ...

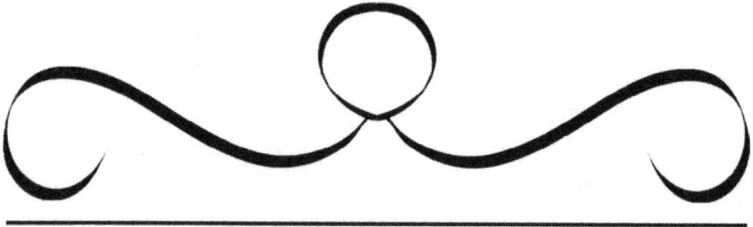

Find the Outlook of Abundance

"When one door closes, another door opens; but we so often look so long and so regretfully upon the closed door, that we do not see the ones which open for us."

Alexander Graham Bell, eminent scientist and inventor

You must embrace the true abundance of the world to get to your best performance. No matter what happens, your ship has not sailed: New ships are constantly coming into port for you. Opportunities are constantly springing up around you. If you live with a narrow perspective of worry and fear, then you won't see them as they arrive.

You may have placed so much importance on one performance that you can't imagine failing. But you've got to keep your perspective. Don't put yourself under so much pressure. If you're worried about not being at your best, relax anyway. Mental pressure causes stress, and stress and flow don't mix, just like oil and water.

Even if you are performing in a high-stakes competition, and losing means you're out of the competition, know that there are always opportunities in your future that you can't even see right now. There are thousands of ways your life can work out. From your limited point of view, you can't always see the perfection of the way things can line up for you.

Think back to when you were younger. How did all the things you were worried about work out? From your perspective now, some of them worked out, some didn't. And many didn't turn out like the worst-case scenario in your mind. In any case, those times passed, just as this one will.

Realize that you're standing on this piece of ground on this planet that is spinning in space. Earth is only one of many planets in many galaxies. From this perspective of time and space, this moment is not that big a deal. The sun will come up tomorrow. The waves will lap the shores of this beautiful Earth, and the tides will come and go.

See this moment as a starting place on your journey. Feel the excitement of that fresh start. Wherever you are right now, however much success or failure you have experienced, you are at the start of your journey. That's because you never stop moving toward something bigger, better, different.

Albert Einstein said that you could live as if nothing is a miracle or everything is a miracle. Choose the miracle. The miracle is that you are here and you are alive right now. Don't take that for granted. You get the chance to pour yourself into this moment for your best and highest performance.

Keep your mind fixed on the abundance of this life. Then, to take your performance to the next level, develop the ability to...

Focus Your Mind

"I felt as though I was driving in a tunnel. The whole circuit became a tunnel... I had reached such a high level of concentration that it was as if the car and I had become one. Together we were at the maximum. I was giving the car everything - and vice versa."

Ayrton Senna, Brazilian race car driver

Focusing your mind will lead you to a great performance. You've already done your preparation; now is the time to focus on the present moment to such an extent that you put yourself into a trance. Being in a trance state means you are in the flow of peak performance.

We've all been in trances. You were in a trance when you daydreamed about being in a place you really wanted to be. You are in a trance when you drive home while thinking about something else or talking on the phone. You are paying attention to the conversation while still knowing what is going on around you.

Your mind has an amazing ability to laser focus so that extraneous details fade into the background. It's not that you can't see other drivers on the road, other players on the field or other people in the room—it's that you have a hyper-conscious awareness of whatever part of the process you're in at that moment.

The easiest way to access such powerful focus is to center yourself in the process, all the individual steps that make up your performance. Just focus on that next step, and then the step after that, and the one after that. If you find your mind wandering out of the process, bring it back to the process.

Now is the time to let go of any leftover worry or concern. Let go of your need to be perfect. Let go of your need for your performance to turn out a certain way.

All the other stuff that you think you want—the success, the adulation, the praise—is just a byproduct of your intense focus on each and every step of your process. Let go of all that and just lose yourself in what you're doing. Let everything that's not important recede into the background. Concentrate on the pleasure of doing your best in this moment, in whatever step of your process you're in. Let time stretch out as you sink into the now.

Sunlight focused through a magnifying glass can start a fire. Your focus is the magnifying glass, channeling your energy and power into the task at hand. Imagine the brilliance of you focused in this moment.

Let your mind focus intently on the process so that you can...

Relax Into It

"The main thing to do is relax and let your talent do the work."

Charles Barkley, NBA Hall of Fame basketball player

The key to performing at your peak state is to relax, not to try hard and "make" it happen. Your greatest effort happened during the time and energy it took to prepare you mentally and physically to be right where you are. The hard part is over. Performance, high performance, is the fun part.

Observe the best of the best and you'll see that when it comes time to deliver, they settle into the idea of perfect expression. When the lights get brightest and the pressure is most intense, they relax more and more, taking time first to draw back within themselves, instead of just plowing ahead.

You can't get to your best through sheer effort. There's something about pushing and hard work that is counter-productive to high performance; it downshifts your energy and weakens you when you most need your strength. It's like trying to rev your engine to 60 miles an hour in first gear: It literally puts you in a place where your body is weakened and your mind is dulled.

When it comes time to perform, your effort is like trying to keep yourself under water with your lungs full of air. Fighting to stay underwater goes against your body's natural tendency to float to the top; just relax, and let all of your ability and talent float to the surface.

Do your best to stay relaxed during your performance. Remember, your mind and body influence one another. You can relax your mind by relaxing your body; breathe deeply and lower your shoulders so you are more centered and grounded. Stretch out your fingers to relieve tension. Smile to release feel-good brain chemicals.

As you breathe deeply, imagine yourself doing what you need to do in full detail. That picture of your successful per-formance is already in your brain, and the physical steps or mental answers will flow to you. Submit yourself to that bigger part of you that already knows how to do each step.

Having the performance you really want is about allow-ing the natural expression of your best self to take place. It's about relaxing and trusting that the way will be laid out for you, that it will unfold in perfect timing, in perfect order. You cannot force the perfect performance to happen, or even anything that resembles it. You allow your best per-formance to emerge by relaxing yourself.

Of course, when you relax into your best performance, it helps to know that you can...

Trust Your Brain

"When I do things without any explanation, but just with spontaneity ... I can be sure that I am right."

Federico Fellini, Academy Award-winning film director

The answers and steps that will take you to a successful performance are already in your brain. If all else fails, simply trust your brain. It's already programmed for your success.

Your brain is like a super computer that's constantly learning. You have information embedded deep in your consciousness that will help you succeed. Even if this information is below the level of your conscious awareness, you can trust that you will get guidance when you need it.

A race car driver was saved by knowledge interpreted by his subconscious, automatic brain. He slammed on the brakes just before he turned a corner, where there was a big pileup ahead that he couldn't see. An analysis of the event videos showed that he had picked up information that he was unaware of as he was about to speed around the corner: the body language of the spectators. His computer brain interpreted, in a fraction of a second, the horror in the spectators' gestures and posture. Not knowing why, he slammed on his brakes and saved himself from a possible fiery death.

Just like that driver, you have information that you can access when you need it. Your brain constantly analyzes millions of bits of information in an attempt to enhance your performance. Most of this information is processed in your nonverbal mind, below your conscious awareness. You perceive it as the brilliant idea you get in the shower, or your gut instinct that makes you throw out the playbook when things aren't going as planned. Messages from this part of your brain guide you, using your intuition and impulses, to avoid the obstacles and overcome the challenges that are thrown your way.

In your brain, you have also assimilated and stored all the information from your preparation, including the wisdom you gained from your successes and your failures. That means you already have the wiring you need for success. The hours of practice have created the neural networks in your brain and placed in them the images of your success. Your body and your mind automatically know what to do.

If you have really practiced a lot and you're not a new kid on the block, then these pathways are at a deep level waiting for you to relax and let them take over. Even if you are new to the game and you haven't had as much practice as you'd like, know that your best shot is to relax and let your brain take over. Then all the information you need becomes accessible to you.

It doesn't matter whether the steps are those needed for a successful vocal performance, a winning run on the football field or an inspiring speech. Your amazing brain can guide you to your best performance.

Follow the knowledge you already have. Follow the impulses that you can trust; that you know will lead you in the right direction. Trust yourself, trust that you're in the right place at the right time.

Trusting your brain will lead you to new heights of performance. It will also help you get away from the worrying and trying hard so you can just...

Be Here Now

"You must live in the present, launch yourself on every wave, find your eternity in each moment. Fools stand on their island of opportunities and look toward another land. There is no other land; there is no other life but this."

Henry David Thoreau, Essayist, Poet and Philosopher

All of your power to perform is here right now. Your best performance comes when you are mindful of each moment, when you allow each moment to catapult you into the next.

Think back to when you were a child and you were in the midst of delicious play: Time stood still as you gobbled up each moment of fun. Time stretched and expanded into eternity. Each minute blended into the next as you easily surrendered to the pleasure and joy of just being there. Maybe you were outside climbing trees or in the basement playing with swords or dolls. There was no thought of when the moment would end. There was no measuring of that moment to see if you could get a better moment. There was just you, drenched in that moment like a flower in rain, loving being there. That incredible feeling of presence in the moment is what you need to recapture now for your top performance.

Where you are right now is where you are right now. It is enough. You are enough. The power is in being fully here now. You're not over there, split off from yourself and analyzing your performance. You're not focused on the past, saying, "I should have prepared better." You're not in the future, worried about the outcome. Imagine the power of *you*, condensed into this moment.

Connecting to this moment is like driving at night. The headlights of your car help you see only the five or ten feet in front of you—but that's all you need. You don't need to turn until you get to the fork in the road, so just focus now on what's in front of you. Look at your surroundings. Notice the colors. Feel your feet on the floor or your weight on the chair. Feel the joy of performing.

The side benefit of being so connected to the moment is that you feel greater fulfillment. If you're only happy when you've won the game or gotten the deal, then you're living in a barren wasteland. What you want is to be your best in each moment of your performance. That way you feel fulfilled no matter the outcome.

This kind of fulfillment means you don't have to win the trophy. Real satisfaction comes from following your process, from enjoying each moment. No one can take that kind of fulfillment away from you. You've just given yourself the best prize of all: enjoyment of the moment, no matter whether you're on top or not.

A masterful performance is the combination of many mastered moments. Don't try to get to the end and jump into the results—you are here to enjoy the process of performance, even more than the outcome. Sink into the moment and let each moment catapult you into the next.

Now you're in the zone. Soak it up and...

Get Into Flow

"Flow is being completely involved in an activity for its own sake. The ego falls away. Time flies. Every action, movement, and thought follows inevitably from the previous one, like playing jazz."

Mihaly Csikszentmihalyi, author of Flow: The Psychology of Optimal Experience

When you are in flow, you can accomplish great physical or mental feats even while your mind is empty and quiet. As you let go of thought, you submit yourself to a deeper part of you and allow it to control your experience. This older, more primitive brain is responsible for leading you to your best performance. Quieting your mind helps you access information so your brain and body act together and more efficiently.

Being in flow feels the same whether you're an athlete, an artist, or a salesperson. You feel time passing effortlessly and slowly as the richness of each moment expands into the next. You move from moment to moment in perfect timing, with no concerns, no worries.

As time slows, things around you become more vivid, and your senses are heightened. In sports, balls seem larger and slow down even while traveling at great speeds. In sales, you pick up on your prospects' feelings and hear the emotion behind their words. In giving a speech, the silence becomes deafening as your audience leans forward for your next words.

When you're in flow you have the feeling that everything is going just right. If you're a salesperson, you have a magical day where you close every sale. If you're an athlete, your body moves gracefully and effortlessly. If you're speaking before a group, you pick up on your audience's feelings and inspiring words come to you in perfect timing and sequence. If you're an actor, you become the character and connect to your most powerful performance.

Your mind is empty and quiet as you release the hold that your useless chatter has on you, shifting you off-center.

Let go of thought, especially of any comparison, and center yourself in the moment. You're not in somebody else's head, wondering how they think you're doing, if your performance is going well. Leave your evaluation of your performance until after you perform. Now, you just flow.

You may feel connected to an unlimited source of power, to forces greater than yourself, and you easily receive the guidance you need. Some performers have described flow as being connected to God, a feeling that allows them to perform divinely at times.

Finding flow doesn't have to be hard. You were born in flow, and as a child you experienced it often. You were completely absorbed in each delicious moment flowing into another. Now you want to access that childlike ability to let time stand still so that each moment blends into the next. Let go of worry and fear. Feel the delight and pleasure of the focused concentration of flow.

Feel the joy of flowing through your best performance in this moment.

You now have everything you need for your best performance. Stay in this space, and enjoy your performance as it unfolds with absolute perfection.

Epilogue:

Checking in with David

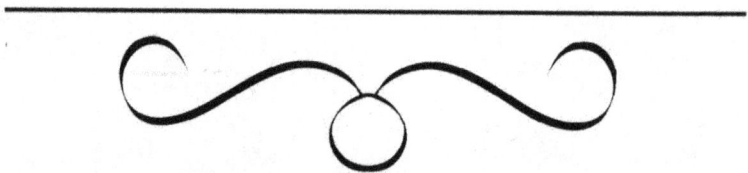

David looked out at the hundreds of salespeople, at the mid- and top-level management, all gathered in the dining room for the annual convention. It was exciting to see people representing so many different countries. He could hardly believe how different he felt from the same time a year ago, when he was sitting on the same stage and practically shaking in his shoes.

All the speeches he had given to the different divisions in his company had helped him learn to trust himself more. There wasn't a single moment he could point to when things clicked and fell into place, but somewhere along the way, somewhere on a stage in Topeka (or was it in Berlin?) he had finally learned to relax. He let go of the worry about how his speech compared to that of other speakers. He didn't feel a renewed sense of confidence because he had prepared more for this talk, because he hadn't. He was re-laxed because he had found that place deep within where he connected to the hidden wellspring of his power. He gave no thought to how it might sound to the audience; in fact, he no longer cared whether anyone at the convention even remembered the stuttering speaker from a year ago.

David slowed his breathing and felt his body relax even more as he quietly waited for the end of the emcee's intro-duction. Colors appeared brighter, and time slowed. It felt strange to be so concentrated and focused in the moment, yet so detached from the outcome.

After his introduction, he strode to the podium. He looked out at the audience and felt the calm assurance of knowing that he would speak eloquently and authentically. He rel-ished the feeling of expansion spreading inside him as he connected to the present moment and to the story he had

75

to share. Only he could tell this story, and he would tell it in his own way.

The chatter in the room stopped as his resonant voice caught their attention. His powerful first words flowed out with ease. "I'm here to talk about hope, because hope is belief in what is still unseen. And a year ago we had no hope of turning this situation around." The measured confidence and cadence of his words silenced the clatter of silverware, and people turned their chairs around to better hear him. David began to feel that delightful sense of momentum as the words and phrases he had practiced flowed smoothly, joined by inspired ideas that seemed to emerge out of the ether.

David felt as though a deeper part of himself was guiding him in his speech. As he spoke, he felt the audience responding on a gut level to his honesty and authenticity as he openly shared his team's early struggles. He spoke passionately about his vision that had inspired and motivated them to unmatched success.

The energy in the room was palpable as he wrapped up his speech, the silence that greeted his last words deafening. Then, applause erupted as people burst from their seats in a standing ovation. David basked a little in the attention, but what he was most proud of was how he felt during his speech. He felt that he had put his best foot forward, that he had really delivered at a time when the company needed him.

Most of all, he felt a sense of satisfaction that came from knowing he could really be himself up there. And his satisfaction grew as he finally felt, within every cell of his being, what it meant to bring his best self to the performance.

He'd given other speeches, but in this one he'd been so in the moment, so in flow, that he'd called everyone in the room to a grander vision of themselves. He'd delivered, and not only on his own promise.

This time, he had delivered hope.

Acknowledgements

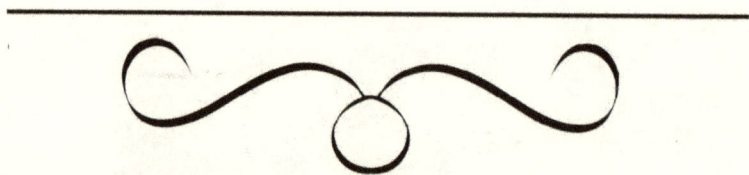

N o book comes together without the help and support of many people. We would like to express our deepest appreciation for those who have helped make this book possible. A thousand thanks go out to all the performers and thought leaders whose shoulders we stand on (and whose insightful quotes we borrowed). Also, we want to thank Bill Caskey and Bryan Neale, who helped shape our understanding of detachment and who have taught us a lot about the inner game of selling.

Thanks to Lynn Stratton for your amazing work editing our book; you sharpened our ideas and helped make the book come to life. Our deepest appreciation goes out to Diane Waybright for your graphic art help. Jordan Perry, thank you for giving us the inspired idea of using Hermes on the cover. Marcus Williams, thank you for capturing what we wanted to see for our very own Hermes and for making it even better than we could have imagined. Also, we want to thank Dawn Nocera for providing wonderful feedback and for your constant support; you are a true friend.

And lastly, we'd like to thank our amazing family. Specifically, thank you David Matthews-Morgan for your technical expertise, for helping us with the cover layout, and for your wonderful input on the book itself. Aaron Matthews-Morgan: Thank you for all your artistic input on the cover and for your feedback on the manuscript. Elissa: Thanks for always being there for us! We could not ask for more loving partners on this journey of co-creation.

About the Authors

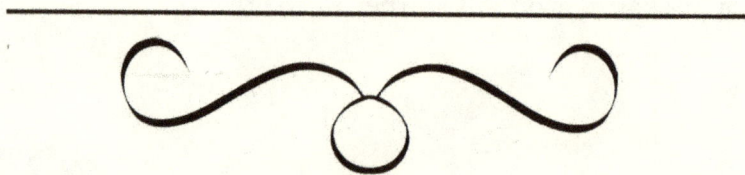

Nita Matthews-Morgan, PhD has a life-long fascination with the brain and its effect on learning and high performance. This passion led her to become a psychologist and has guided much of her career.

She is the co-founder of Learn Your Brain, a company that helps individuals and teams achieve peak performance.

Prior to founding Learn Your Brain, Nita taught at the University of Georgia and was the Director of the Torrance Center for Creative Studies and Talent Development.

Josh Matthews-Morgan has experienced performance from many angles—as a speaker, athlete, musician, actor and salesperson.

Josh is the co-founder of Learn Your Brain, a company that helps individuals and teams develop the mental programming for peak performance.

Josh and Nita are the creators of two cutting-edge online training programs, which can be found at: www.learnyourbrain.com

Excelerate teaches individuals and teams principles of peak-performance from brain science and positive psychology.

Tools for Transformation teaches strategies and tools from brain science for identifying and deleting limiting beliefs and emotional blocks.

www.ingramcontent.com/pod-product-compliance
Lightning Source LLC
Chambersburg PA
CBHW022127280326
41933CB00007B/577